He was hungry. He could see leaves and fruit on the other side of the river.

3

Now in the river there was a crocodile.

The crocodile was hungry too.
He wanted to eat Little Mouse Deer.

5

When Crocodile saw Little Mouse Deer he said, "Do you want to get to the other side of the river?"

7

Little Mouse Deer did not want Crocodile to help him.
"Crocodile will not help me," he said to himself.
"He will eat me."

9

So Little Mouse Deer said, "The king wants me to count how many crocodiles there are in the river."

11

"Make a line in the river," said Little Mouse Deer. "Then I can count how many crocodiles there are."

12

13

14

So all the crocodiles made a line in the river. Then Little Mouse Deer jumped on the first crocodile. As he jumped Little Mouse Deer said, "One."

Then he jumped on the next crocodile. As he jumped Little Mouse Deer said, "Two."

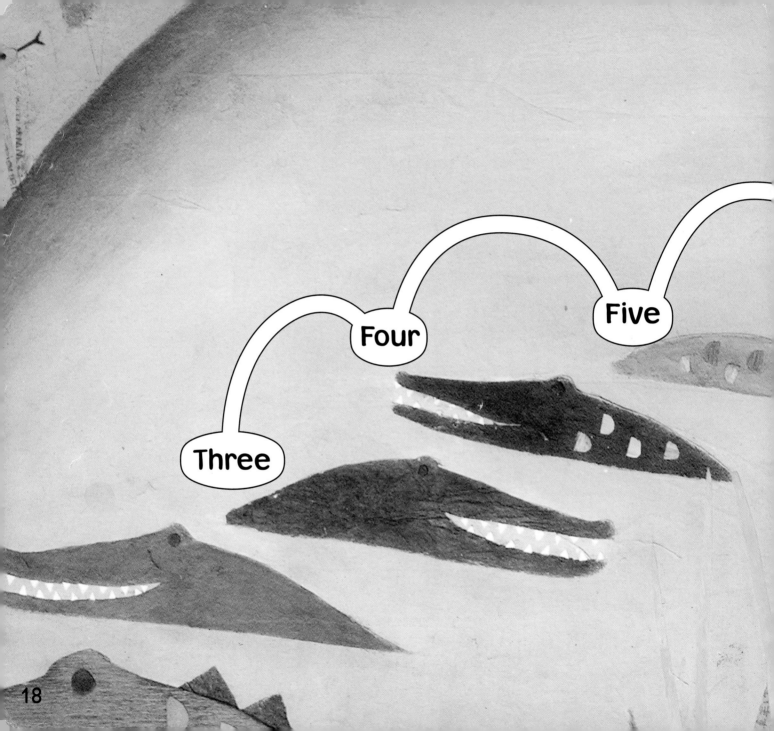

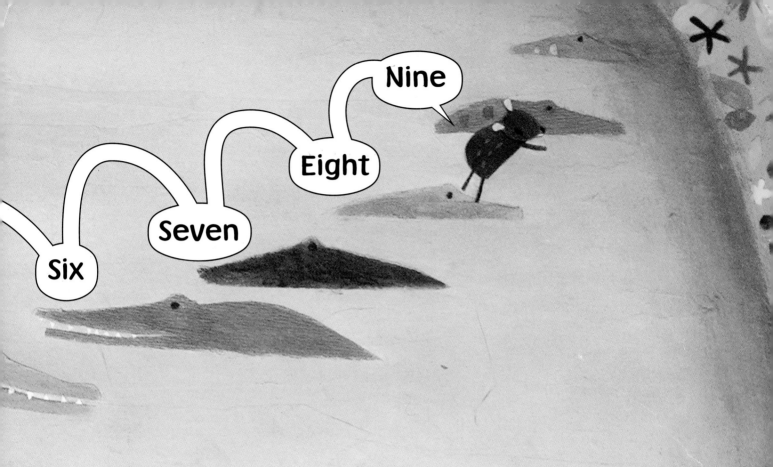

Then he jumped on the next crocodile and the next and the next. As he jumped he said, "Three, four, five, six, seven, eight, nine..."

When he jumped on the last crocodile
he said, "Ten!"

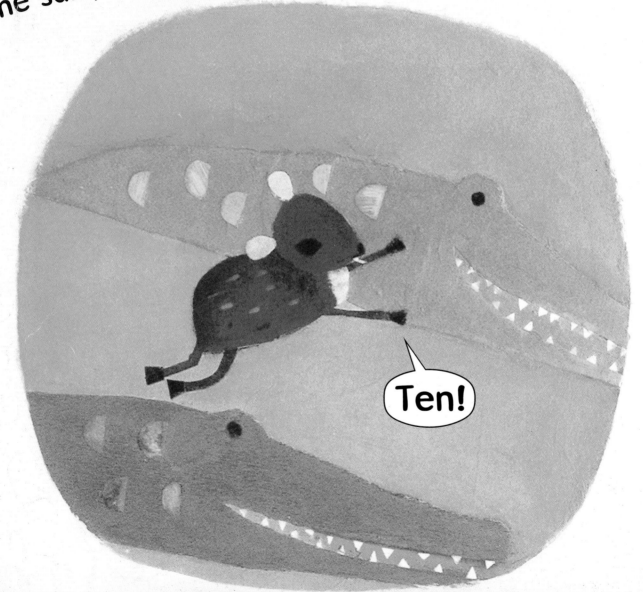

By now, Little Mouse Deer was on the other side of the river.

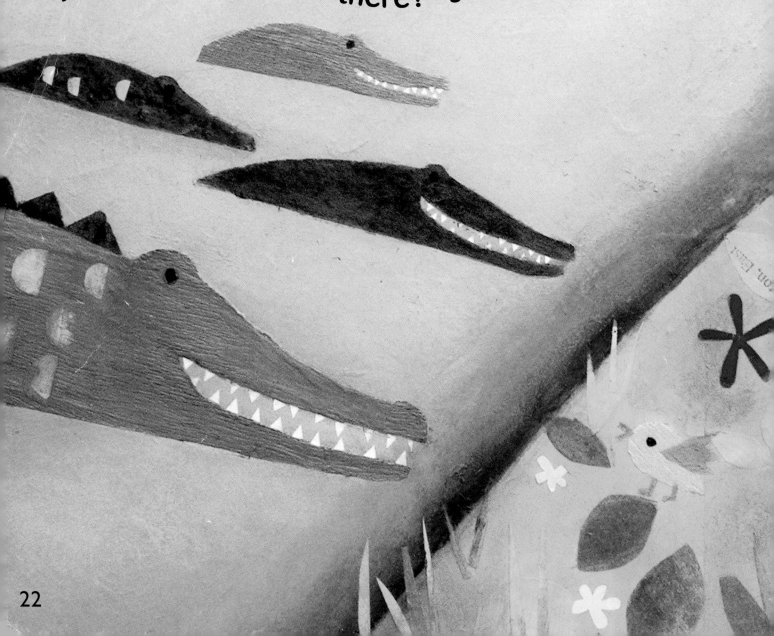

"How many of us are there?" said Crocodile.

"There are ten," said Little Mouse Deer, "and they are all like you - foolish!"

Then Little Mouse Deer went off to eat leaves and fruit but Crocodile was still hungry.